THE
SPECTATOR
CARTOON BOOK

Edited by
Michael Heath

The Spectator (1828) Limited

Published by The Spectator (1828) Ltd
56 Doughty Street, London WC1N 2LL

© The Spectator, 2005

Designed and typeset by The Spectator
production@spectator.co.uk

Printed and bound in Great Britain by Clays Ltd, St Ives Plc

A CIP catalogue record for this book is available from
the British Library.

ISBN: 0 9551173 0 5

'They've all gone outside for a fag.'

'Lesbos must be further north — we seem to have stumbled on Asbos.'

'Blasted townies!'

'Lay lady lay . . .'

'I'm sorry, the bone is off.'

'I can remember when he was only the village idiot.'

'Push!'

'You've got that Gilchrist woman all wrong —
she doesn't jump into bed with anybody.'

'Go easy on those batteries, junior.'

'Sergeant, find out who's not shoring up the tunnel properly.'

'Wonderful news, we're melting the sodding ice caps!'

'Come in, let me show you around and around and around . . .'

'. . . Turn left, drop down to 30 'til you've passed the
speed camera, gun her back up to 60 through the
village, you'll see the pub on the left — finish on a
hand-brake turn in the car park.'

'It's a video of me stealing the phone.'

BILL PROUD

'I've always said we need strong leadership.'

'I may not know art, but I know what goes over a green sofa.'

'None of us would be here if we could stop at just the one ant . . .'

'Beryl's into Nordic street-walking.'

'... a motor mechanic, how interesting...'

'So I dumped the life coach and got myself a fairy godmother.'

'Let's see . . . I was shot on Law and Order, *died on* E.R.,
and brought back to life on The X Files.'

'I can remember when this was all chimneys.'

'Will you get your eyes tested? You've put the hamster in the fish tank.'

'For chrissake — I slaved over a hot stove for 3 minutes to make that for you. At least try it.'

'Now I wish I hadn't complained about my soup . . .'

*'I'm not talking sweatshop, but can't we get
them to do a little something?'*

*'In the event of an emergency, exits are located
on both sides of the vehicle . . .'*

'I know grandad sometimes forgets your pocket money, darling, but that's not the way to ask.'

'Oh, George — if only I wasn't repulsed by your touch.'

*'I'm Tom and I'll be looking after you this evening even though
it's supposed to be my night off.'*

'Ralph Johnson's worked at Charburger for far less time than you, and already he's Fries Captain.'

'So what's this system you're using to sort out our credit card debts?'

'Pay no attention — our security camera is broken.'

'Pensioners are amazing — they can live on next to nothing for weeks.'

'I will now make your luggage disappear for ever!'

'Congratulations, Doug — from today you can be tried as an adult.'

'You know, it actually pays us to come half way across the galaxy to stock up on booze and fags.'

Binge Crosby

'Look at that! I've already done 10,000 sips on my pedometer.'

'It's a lack-of-water feature.'

'Any skills? Well, I got this far, didn't I?'

'That puts the kibosh on the peace talks.'

Russell.

'Hold on, we're going into a tunnel.'

'I suppose you're seeing more of your dad this way.'

'Don't you hate the gay graffiti you get in public toilets?'

'Damn sirens go off as soon as anyone goes near them.'

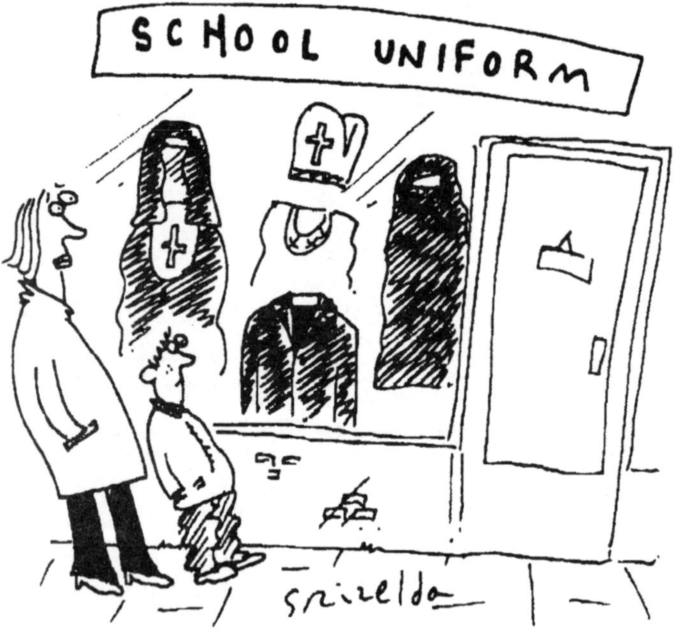
SCHOOL UNIFORM
grizelda

'It's nothing personal, Roger, I just need some space, that's all.'

'Lucy played house-to-house fighting with her doll's houses today.'

'I just feel so safe in my 4WD.'

'Close the store! This carrot's got soil on it!'

'How goes the unstarted symphony?'

Strangers on a British Train

'God, reformed alcoholics are so damned smug.'

'I assume this is tax deductible?'

'I don't approve of building wind farms, they ruin the landscape.'

'It was the last five vodka and cokes, eight champagne cocktails, and six tequila shots that did it.'

'And should you be placed under house arrest,
this is a delightful property to be confined to.'

'I'm five, but I can play three to seven and a half.'

'It's a contemporary update of the children's classic.'

'The more I drink, the more he makes sense.'

'My luggage has gone to Hell.'

'It hasn't all been plain sailing. There were times when we didn't know where our next 4x4 was coming from . . .'

'I'm sorry, Mrs Brown, but you coming here does not make up for your son's truancy.'

'Welcome to the neighbourhood, where've you moved from?'

'I suppose I am ready for marriage — I'm getting awfully tired of sex.'

'And you're to stop frightening the children
with your evacuee stories.'

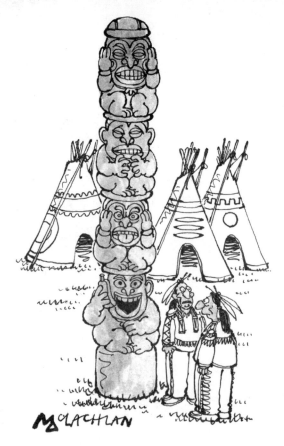

'Well, we have to move with the times.'